THE
T.E. LAWRENCE
POEMS

THE
T.E. LAWRENCE
POEMS

Gwendolyn MacEwen

Mosaic Press/Valley Editions

"Publishers for Canadian Communities"

Canadian Cataloguing in Publication Data

MacEwen, Gwendolyn 1941-
    The T.E. Lawrence Poems

ISBN 0-88962-173-4 (bound). - ISBN 0-88962-172-1 (pbk.)

1. Lawrence, T.E. (Thomas Edward), 1888-1935, in
fiction, drama, poetry, etc. I. Title.

PS8525.E95T22   C811'.54   C82-094506-4
PR9199.3.M242T22

Published by Mosaic Press/Valley Editions
P.O. Box 1032, Oakville, Ont., L6J 5E9, Canada.

Published with the assistance of the Canada Council and the Ontario
Arts Council.

Copyright © Gwendolyn MacEwen, 1982

Second Printing, 1983.

Typeset by Speed River Graphics.
Designed by Doug Frank.
Cover drawing from the
    National Portrait Gallery, London, England
Printed and bound by Les Editions Marquis Ltée.

ISBN 0-88962-173-4 cloth
ISBN 0-88962-172-1 paper

Distributed in the United States by Flatiron Books, 175 Fifth
Avenue, Suite 814, New York, N.Y. 10010, U.S.A.

Distributed in the U.K. by John Calder (Publishers) Ltd., 18 Brewer
Street, London, W1R 4AS, England.

Distributed in New Zealand and Australia by Pilgrims South Press,
P.O. Box 5101, Dunedin, New Zealand.

Mosaic Press, Publishers

FOREWORD

In 1962 I was staying in a hotel in Tiberias, Israel; the tall, white-haired proprietor invited me downstairs one evening and served me syrupy tea and a plate of fruit. He showed me a series of old sepiatone photographs which lined the walls — photographs of blurred riders on camels riding to the left into some uncharted desert just beyond the door. Some of them were signed.

'It's Lawrence, isn't it?' I asked, walking up to one.

'Yes,' said my host, offering me a huge section of an orange. 'I rode with him once a long time ago. I see you always carry a pen and paper to write things down. I thought you'd be interested; I thought you'd like to know.'

These poems were written some twenty years later.

Early versions of some of these poems appeared in *Exile* and *Prism* magazines; others were broadcast on CBC Radio's *Anthology* program. The author would like to thank the Canada Council of the Arts for its support.

CONTENTS

3. *Necessary Evils*: Aftermath 57

1
THE DREAMERS OF THE DAY
For Dahoum

WATER

When you think of it, water is everything. Or rather,
Water ventures into everything and becomes everything.
   It has
All tastes and moods imaginable; water is history
And the end of the world is water also.
           I have tasted water
From London to Miranshah. In France it tasted
Of Crusaders' breastplates, swords, and tunnels of rings
On ladies' fingers.
     In the springs of Lebanon water had
No color, and was therefore all colors,
         outside of Damascus
It disguised itself as snow and let itself be chopped
And spooned onto the stunned red grapes of summer.

For years I have defended water, even though I am told
    there are other drinks.
Water will never lie to you, even when it insinuates itself
Into someone else's territory. Water has style.

Water has no conscience and no shame; water
    thrives on water, is self-quenching.
It often tastes of brine and ammonia, and always
Knows its way back home.

When you want to travel very far, do as the Bedouin do —
Drink to overflowing when you can,
      and then
Go sparingly between wells.

THE PARENTS

Frightened people, they stared into cameras
        and their souls came out in sepiatone.
I can't imagine them doing anything with passion,
But if it is true that the fault of birth rests somehow
        with the child, and I believe it is so,
        then I was the one who led them on to bear me;
I was responsible for all that tossing and heaving,
I the unborn one caused their flesh to itch and burn.

I was the bed on which they lay; their shy and awkward crimes
        were once committed in my name.
Their necessary dark did not deceive me, their furtive
        Victorian midnights did not deceive me.
I was the place they sold their souls in, and now I pay
For every breath I draw with the memory of their shame.

Now it is I who must give birth to them, redeem them
        and restore them to a kind of grace,
        for I carry them around within me endlessly.
Father and Mother, be born in me.

MY MOTHER

In Dublin they called her The Holy Viper; she helped God
      to erase all sins except her own.
Knowing her means I'll never make any woman a mother;
Let them find something else to devour besides
      their own children.
She didn't care for girls in the house, they weren't her.

I never let her see exactly who I was and what I loved,
      for she would understand, and then I
      would have to also. She was illegitimate
      like me; it ran in our blood.

I was a standing civil war for as long as I remember,
Trying to contain both her and my father, and now
      I am a castle that she lays siege to;
      she aspires to its tower.

The Arabs say that Mother Eve is a giant who stands
      three hundred feet tall;
      if I raise myself to my full height
Then I can see her, green and powerful, gazing at me still.

MY FATHER

He never looked at anyone, not even me, like once
On one of those official city mornings, he stepped
       right on my foot in the middle of the road
       and kept on walking into nowhere.

He had inherited enough money for him to sail yachts
And shoot pheasants, and ride hard and drink hard
       until she tamed him with her fairy tales
       about God, and how He loved the sinner,
Not the sin. I wonder what he thought of his five
       little bastards. It was impossible to tell.

Now I'm very much like that country gentleman, in that
I can talk to you for hours without for a moment revealing
       that I don't have a clue who you are;
I never look at a man's face and never recognize one;
       I have never been sure of the color of my eyes.

Sometimes he looked so lost that I wanted to show him
The way back home, but the house had become a place
       of thunder; it stared at us with square,
       unseeing eyes, and I never knew why
He went to her in that permanent, resounding dark.

I suppose he might have been a lion of a man, but
When you castrate a lion, all its mane falls out and
       it mews like a cat. Imagine, he was afraid
       of everything; I, of nothing — (my key
       opened all the houses on the street, I thought).

Once as a boy I asked someone if a statue I stared at
Was alive. They said no, but they were wrong. It was.

OUR CHILD WHICH ART IN HEAVEN

The child leads the parents on to bear him; he demands
            to be born. And I sense somehow that God
Is not yet born; I want to create Him.

If everything were finished, and we could say
            we'd given birth to stars, if we could say
Give over, it's done — all would be wild, and fair.

But it is not yet over; it has not yet begun.

God is not yet born, and we await the long scream
            of His coming. We want the water to break
So we can say: *In the Beginning was the Word.*

Meanwhile, if one must die for something,
            there's nothing like a cross
            from which to contemplate the world.

THE LEGITIMATE PRINCE

I was a flea in the legitimate prince's bed, the bed
Of he-who-was-not-me, he who had the real birthright.
He wore noble clothes,
                          and saved every damsel in distress
Within a hundred miles. His eyes and his scabbard shone.

He-who-was-not-me showed no mercy and no fear for anything.
Lies glanced off his sword — shot light.
                                        Terror swooned;
He answered to no one, and claimed the world as his own.

He never looked anyone in the eye for fear they would fall
Into the well of his gaze and drown there, thrashing around
             like the fools, the pipsqueaks they were,
And he wanted to spare them.
                          All colours admired him, God
             admired him, God how I longed to become him.

But I was born on the wrong side of the bed, which made me
Prince of Nothing, and I fell off the edge of it into Hell.

MY BROTHERS

They were all very different from me, aside from the fact
That their hair parted down the left, and mine
        down the right; we were clever, I think,
        and our several lives branched away
        from the common root that was *she.*
Her dreaded love both nurtured and deprived us, and we
Looked for worlds that existed beyond her.

Arnie became an archaeologist and started a museum in Ghana,
        (little Arnie who I loved most dearly).
Frank and Will were killed in the war. (Will, even Will,
        who was tall and beautiful).
Bob, whose face shone from the inside like a lamp, Bob
        who was lost in Christ,
        went to China with Mother
        to teach them there about God.

MY HALF-SISTERS

Like the legitimate prince, they were legitimate princesses,
        (my father was actually married to their mother) —
And I, their bastard half-brother, used to imagine them
Crochetting doilies and toiling over impossible needlepoint
            in shadowy alcoves where their purple dresses
            fluttered, and their powerful and secret minds
            made mock of me and my bastard brothers.

One half of them was one half of me; I never could fathom
            what that meant. They were forbidden to me
            by blood, yet I felt them lurking, waiting
            to devour me just beyond my door.
My ghostly half-sisters, beautiful and cruel, were fond
Of tea and blueberry scones at ten past five, talked
            incessantly of me, and slowly got older.

Now I think they might drop a stitch when someone comes—
            a visitor or a casual friend— and asks them
            if their half-brother is really the uncrowned
King of Arabia. I wonder what they say to him,
            those odd, uncanny women,
            my twilight sisters, guarded by unicorns.

IT WAS ONLY A GAME

As children my brothers and friends and I used to play
A very simple game. The good guys, knights in armour,
        would lay siege to a castle held by the
        bad guys who were holding some of our
        good guys.
                We of course had to free the
        good guys from them, the wicked ones.
Or—

        We could be the bad ones and hold the
        fortress against the onslaught of the
        good ones who were coming to get more
        of their good ones from us.

Maybe it wasn't such a simple game. In any case,
Those hostages of high cities, prisoners of citadels
        were real, and the castles containing them
        were real, because we deemed them so.
We the saviours were rewarded with gold rings and huge
Banquets with boars' heads stuffed with fruit, oranges
Studded with cloves, and wine all over the place.

The wild clumsy summers of our play succumbed to Fall,
And then to long sullen winters.
                        I dreamed of having
Millions of people expressing themselves through me,
Of being the saviour of a whole race, of rescuing
A whole people from tyranny. Those were the tender,
        obscene dreams of my childhood.

Alone at night in the breathing garden, I needed horses,
And limitless space. Everything awaited me — the world
        and the world beyond.

I didn't see the enemy outside, scaling the garden walls.
How easily are we overcome, how cleverly are we destroyed.

IN BED

One should only live in the future or the past,
In Utopia or The Wood Beyond the World, I said,
        but I had this Mission; it devoured
        my waking moments, and forced the present
        upon me like a storm.

I had a brass-rubbing of a dead Crusader on the ceiling
And when sometimes, in satin midnights,
                        my flesh crawled
With unspeakable desires, and the wind teased
The silly trees,
        and I knew myself to be
Just one step short of perfect — I'd lie and stare
At that ridiculous hero,
              his lurid body eaten by worms,
Night after night above me.

WORDS FROM THE PREACHER AT OXFORD

Let me implore you, my
                young friends,
                        not
To imperil your immortal souls upon a pleasure,
                              which

so far as I am credibly informed

Lasts
    less then
            one and three-quarter
Minutes.

JANET

I think I loved her; we played together as children,
    then suddenly we both grew up, and I
    stood there and asked her to marry me
    because that seemed the thing to do.

She said no, even though I had been a perfect gentleman;
    I know I was a perfect gentleman because
    I never in my life touched her.

Then she was going to marry somebody else, and she
    asked me to give her away. I said no,
    I would look like an ass; I was too damn short
    to walk down the aisle with her.

ANIMAL SPIRITS

Is it true, then, that one fears all that one loves?
These spirits are my awful companions; I can't tell
          anyone when they move in me.
They are so mighty they are unclean; it is the end
Of cleanliness; it is the great crime.

I can only kill them by becoming them. They are all
I have ever loved or wanted; their hooves and paws
          smell of honey and trodden flowers.

Those who do not know me sip their bitter coffee
          and mutter of war. They do not know
          I am wrestling with the spirits
          and have almost won. They do not know
I am looking out from the camels' eyes, out
          from the eyes of the horses.

It is vile to love them; I will not love them.
                              Look—
My brain is sudden and silent as a wildcat.
                              Lord,
Teach me to be lean, and wise. Nothing matters,
          nothing *matters*.

THE CHILD AND THE CATHEDRAL

It was in the white light of a dreadful afternoon
           that I saw the child. She wore a bright
White dress and was playing with a ball in front
Of the cathedral. I knew
                  she was animal; in my hatred
Of animals I began to balance her
                      against the cathedral.

If I had to sacrifice one of them, I asked myself —
           which would it be?
                  I knew it was
The cathedral. I would destroy it to save her.

Another time I swerved at sixty miles an hour
To save some damned little bird that dashed itself out
           against my side-car. Why did it have to
Kill itself against *me*, for God's sake, why *me*?

Don't they know their existence wounds me, don't
They know I am the victim of such loveliness
           I want to die in it and cannot?
Don't they know the hatred and fear and pity go on and on
And turn into love, horrible love that bashes
           its brains out against the light?

FURTHERMORE

I hate noise and fear animal spirits
                              (as I have said)
And like warmth and smooth things and music
         (although it hurts me)
And books and abstract talk and color, lots of color
And cats and camels, because they chase their appetites.

(The excellent cat licks an eclair all down its middle
And turns it into a dugout canoe.)

         Also —
My favorite color is scarlet,
My favorite dish is bread and water,
My favorite music is Mozart,
My favorite author is William Morris,
My favorite character in history is nobody,
My favorite place is London,
And my greatest pleasure is sleep.

Now you know me.

THE WATER-BEARER

On a hill at Carcemish which is in Mesapotamia, which is
        Between-the-Rivers,
We dug up the bones and artifacts of ancient strangers,
You and your donkey lugging buckets of water
        back and forth over many thousands of years,
While I made notes about absolutely everything, and
        wrote long letters home.

You watered the mules and camels and nothing was ever
Too pretty or tiresome that you couldn't make mad and
        silly fun of it;
                everything admired you.
The animals admired you because you had a splendid
        disregard for man that even they
        could not achieve. And a dark and secret love
That only they could achieve.

When it was too hot, we swam, and then the river
Released us and found its way back home.

They called you Darkness although your skin was fair;
I gave you a camera and taught you how to explore
        the darkness that lived behind light;
You said you would take pictures of the whole world.

Water-bearer, you gave everything and asked nothing
        in return. We dreamed that one day
        the ghosts of your ancestors would arise
        and tell to us wonderful Hittite secrets;
But we had forgotten that your name meant also
        the darkness of water before Creation;
        we did not know that you would one day drown
In the dark water of your own lungs.

I loved you, I believe. It was before the horror.

NAKED PEOPLE

Do you really like naked women? I asked my sculptor friend.
They express so little.
                                    I've never thought twice or even
Once of a naked woman. Does that mean I'm abnormal, or
A unicorn who's strayed among sheep, and what on earth
Does *that* mean?

Kurdish ladies with awful thin lips once ripped almost all
                my clothes off, outside Carcemish
                and giggling, felt me up all over.
I wonder if they found me beautiful. Their jewellery
Was blue and silver. I wore no jewels.

I carved you naked in limestone for the roof of the house
In Carcemish, but your nakedness only made you
                more secret and inviolable than before.
For a while I thought the stone would contain you, but
                nothing contained you, not even
The bold bright clothes you wore, not even the whole
Width of the sky, and the length of the bright river.

It was as though you assumed
                                the world for a while;
Then you fell still, naked and chill and wondering.

THE DESERT

Only God lives there in the seductive Nothing
That implodes into pure light. English makes Him
        an ugly monosyllable, but Allah breathes
A fiery music from His tongue, ignites the sands,
        invents a terrible love that is
The very name of pain.

The desert preserves Him
        as the prophets found Him, massive and alone.
They went there, into that awful Zero
                to interpret Him,
        for Himself to know, for He said: Help me,
I am the One who is alone, not you. Tell Me who I am.

Camels lean into the desert, lost in some thought
        so profound it can only be guessed. When
Will God invent man? When
            will the great dream end?
My skin crawls with a horrible beauty in this
        Nothingness, this Everything —

I fall to my knees in the deep white sand, and my head
        implodes into pure light.

THE ABSOLUTE ROOM

We came to a place which was the center of ourselves
        in the desert between Aleppo and Hama;
We came to this Roman place where a hundred scents
        were built somehow right into the walls.
So the old man and the boy led us through courts
        of jasmine, and many other flowers, then

Into this great hall where all the scents slayed
        each other, and were still, and all
We breathed was pure desert air.

                    We call
        this room the sweetest of them all,
You said.
        And I thought: *Because there is nothing here.*

I knew then that you possessed nothing of me, and I
        possessed nothing of you, Dahoum.
We were wealthy and stuffed with a wondrous nothing
        that filled the room and everything around.

You looked into my eyes, the windows to my soul,
        and said that because they were blue
You could see right through them, holes in my skull,
        to the quiet, powerful sky beyond.

EXCAVATING IN EGYPT

Nobody knows how cold the nights can get in a land
Where sun is lord of the morning. It comes at you
        like a sword, the cold, and lays its side
        along your ribs;
                there the flat steel sings
And you shiver under it, waiting for the dawn.

By day in Kafr Ammar we found trinkets of a people
Who lived there before the pharaohs — odd jewels
        and sad little things that could have been
        gods, or toys;
        Whatever they were, one played with them.

By night we grew fearful of these things; as the air
        grew more and more chill
        we gathered them up and returned to the tents,
        smelling of a thousand sweet, pungent spices,

Having wrapped ourselves in the funeral-cloths of the dead.

THE STORY OF A STONE

There is a stone in the blue fields of midnight,
And finally the stone is its own story; the stone
       will always tell you nothing about itself.

What lives inside the stone?
              Miracles, strange light.

The stone is a superior star; it invents itself,
       makes history, pursues itself down
The same hill forever, or just lies there being
A stone.

I have been sitting here for three hours under this
Handsome tree, trying to get blood
              out of this stone,
But it lies there contemplating itself in a state
      of perfect bliss.
           The sky abounds with silence,
And everything is proceeding slowly, very surely,
Somewhere.

THUNDER-SONG

Two musicians played before the storm broke; one played
Wind-song, wind in the dry valley grass;
                                                    one played
            dark, blind music on two strings. They both
Sang of war and love and death — what else is there
            to sing for?

Then came the armies of rain, wave after wave of it,
And a murderous blue lightning which brought the stones
            to life in the courtyard outside.
                                        Two lions
            on a pedestal laughed and laughed at us, with
            blue rain slobbering down their jaws, and then

Came the god, striding along an inscription towards the door.

The first musician controlled the thunder with his pipe
And the second explored the spaces in between
            the statements of the light.
                                        In the place we were,
The place between twin rivers, Babylon, all was articulate
And utterly real.
                        Then the storm subsided and the pipe wept
At its passing. I knew that if ever I died it would be thus:

A helmetted seven-foot god coming quietly in blue light
Towards me.

A FAREWELL TO CARCEMISH

Time contains me as once your eyes contained me, utterly.

I leave you to guard the site,
                            its layers of history.
I am moving back to the world,
                            I exit sideways, slide
From your eyes.
                    No one is with you. The sightless desert
Is with you.
                    Wind from the sun
                                    stirs your black robes.
Maktub: It is written.

He is only dangerous who dreams by day.

2
SOLAR WIND
The War

APOLOGIES

I did not choose Arabia; it chose me. The shabby money
That the desert offered us bought lies, bought victory.
          What was I, that soiled Outsider, doing
Among them? I was not becoming one of them, no matter
What you think. They found it easier to learn my kind
          of Arabic, than to teach me theirs.
And they were all mad; they mounted their horses and camels
          from the right.

But my mind's twin kingdoms waged an everlasting war;
The reckless Bedouin and the civilized Englishman
          fought for control, so that I, whatever I was,
Fell into a dumb void that even a false god could not fill,
          could not inhabit.

The Arabs are children of the idea; dangle an idea
In front of them, and you can swing them wherever.
          I was also a child of the idea; I wanted
          no liberty for myself, but to bestow it
Upon them. I wanted to present them with a gift so fine
          it would outshine all other gifts in their eyes;
          it would be *worthy*. Then I at last could be
Empty.

You can't imagine how beautiful it is to be empty.
Out of this grand emptiness wonderful things must surely
          come into being.
When we set out, it was morning. We hardly knew
That when we moved we would not be an army, but a world.

ALI

Among the four sons of Sharif Hussein, in whose veins
Flowed the blood of the Prophet, I sought the man
who would lead his people against the Turks
        and on into Damascus.
Zeid was too young; Abdullah was jovial and too clever
For his own good.
           And then there was Ali, pious and clean
To a fault, Ali who loved beautiful things above all.

Often at dusk I'd catch him secretly smiling
        over the sheep heads that were also smiling
        on their beds of rice. He knew that I knew
He had thoughts too beautiful to be told. And once,
        he wrote to his Hashemite father, saying
How could his men advance on the enemy, without swords
        in scabbards of beaten gold?

Ali was not well; a delicate illness governed him
And made him a visitor, not a citizen of the world,
        and he talked much to his horses,
        and fondled them, which was something
I could never stand. It is not good to love and honor
        anything overmuch, as I have said.

Yet when I said goodbye to him once, we walked away
In separate directions, knowing that we understood
One another far more than either of us could say,
        and we were brothers just visiting the world.

FEISAL

He was standing in a doorway waiting for me, all white,
Framed in black, with the light
                        slanting down on him—
            a heavenly weapon.
Of the ten thousand and thirty-seven words for *sword*
            in Arabic, his name meant one:
The sword flashing downward in the stroke.

My lord Feisal, the man I had come to Arabia to seek,
Had a calm Byzantine face which, like an ikon,
            was designed to reveal nothing. Many times,
            I learned later, he had watched his men
            tortured by the Turks, and his black eyes
With their quiet fire did not flinch or turn away.

When he was at rest, his whole body was watching,
And when he moved, he floated over the earth, a prince.
            Once when I saw him, dark against the sun,
            its haze all gold through the silk of his *aba*,
I knew I would have sold my soul for him, joyfully.

And how do you like our place here in Wadi Safra?
            he asked me, looking off to one side of me,
            as though an angel stood there, listening.
Well, I said: *but it is far from Damascus.*

Later, when we rode northward into the dream that was his
And mine, he paid some of the men by letting them dip
            their hands into a box of gold sovereigns,
            and keep, not counting, all one hand could hold.
To reassure the others, he carried around false money —
Boxes of stones that rattled like silver and gold —
And we carried in our knapsacks the paper secrets
            that were war, the bundles of rotting letters,
            the green figs, the promises, the lies.

No matter what happened they would always adore him —
            the prince whose name was a sword —
And I would follow my lord Feisal from Wadi Safra
            to the ends of the earth.

VISUAL PURPLE

Is a substance in the eye necessary for night vision.
By day, in the blonde light of those deserts,
        the villages predicted each other;
        they were districts of the mind.
More than one man who served us lamb and rice at dusk
        was blind.

I speak of where I've been, not where I'm going.
Time is a myth, a silver slit in space. With you
        I entered a wise and handsome darkness.
We took the sweet road to Somewhere, along the dusty
        parallels of my dream and of yours.

Here are the cities of my spirit as I remember them
In time:
        Mecca, Jidda, Rabegh, Yenbo, Un Lej, Wejh,
        Akaba, Ma'an, Beersheba, Jerusalem, Amman,
        Deraa, Damascus.

But only by day were they real cities.
                        By night
They were the kingdoms that lay in one another's mind—
Our secret, intact kingdoms shot with purple light,
Unconquered and unconquerable.

AUDA

Auda was loud and lovely and his honor was more than gold
Among the Howeitat. No one could sing or ride like him;
        he ate the desert. He had slain seventy-five Arabs
        and Turks beyond counting, and the enemy was never
So lovely to him as when its life was his to take or give.
His heart was so huge it yearned towards the defeated one;
        I think at the moment he killed, he loved him.

As we sat in a circle at dinner around a pyramid of lamb
        and rice, he'd offer me the choicest chunks,
        and I'd give him some awful lump of guts
        in return, for Auda loved a damn good joke.
I made him laugh by telling his own stories better than he,
Of wild campaigns and how many men he killed — but always
Blood was blood; it was always red, only growing darker
        when it staled.

One night at dinner he got mad and stomped outside the tent
        and tore his false teeth from his mouth
        and did a little jig on them upon a rock
        because they offended him; a Turk had made them.
Later, when the night grew cold and we drank coffee,
I remember him musing: *Why do Westerners want everything?*
        Behind our few stars we can see God
        who is not behind your millions.
I said: *We want the world's end, Auda.*

He had twenty-eight wives, but only one son alive,
And one night I came across him in his tent, fucking
        one of his new wives, a jolly girl.
        I was shocked that he took that awful comical
        process of life so seriously. *Why, Auda?*
        That's all I asked him — *why?*
And he said he wanted sons. Why did Auda want sons, why
Did anyone want sons, why did I have to walk in on Auda,
Magnificent Auda, and see him riding a woman like a fool?

Her lips were blue and her breasts were pointing to heaven;
She was enduring that unbearable humiliation to get a child.
      She ran away, what else could she do,
      and the wind whistled down the wadi
      and the exhausted camels roared.
Afterwards, I laughed at Auda and he laughed a little too,
      but he looked at me sideways and I knew
      that he knew something I didn't know
      and have never known.
It was colder than ever that night in Wadi Ruum.

WHAT IT'S LIKE

What is it like to believe in everything?

To believe in everything is like the Howeitat remedy
For snakebite.

Bind a plaster of snakeskin on the wound, and then
Read aloud certain chapters of the Koran
Until the victim dies.

THE VIRGIN WARRIOR

When we rested between marches, I read Aristophanes
In the original Greek. I also had
                                Morte d'Arthur, and
The Oxford Book of English Verse.
                                Then came the day
            of the camel charge; we surged forward, swords
            raised like exclamation marks, and
            purple banners flying.
When the enemy became real, I got terribly excited
            and shot my camel through the head
            by accident, flew to the ground
And lay there with her as the army leapt over us,

Thinking, in lines as long as a camel's stride, of Kipling.

THE MIRAGE

This is the desert, as I promised you.
        There are no landmarks, only
Those you imagine, or those made by rocks
        that fell from heaven.

Did you ever know where you were going?
        Am I as invisible to you
As you always were to me, fellow traveller?
        You are not here for nothing.

There are no easy ways of seeing, riding
        the waves of invisible seas
In marvellous vessels which are always
        arriving or departing.

I have come to uncover the famous secrets
        of earth and water, air and fire.
I have come to explore and contain them all.
        I am an eye.

I need tons of yellow space, and nothing
        in the spectrum is unknown to me.
I am the living center of your sight; I draw for you
        this thin and dangerous horizon.

THE MEETING

In the afternoon, Nuri Shaalan appeared, with Trad
and Khalid, Faris, Durzi, and the Khaffaji. Auda
abu Tayi arrived, with Mohammed el Deilann, also
Fahad and Adhub, the Zebn leaders, with ibn Bani,
the chief of the Serahin, and ibn Genj of the Ser-
diyeh.

And then the meeting began.

DAOUD AND FARRAJ

They were my heavenly twins, although they were not
       brothers, but wise and rowdy souls who seized
       their love and joy whenever they desired,
       whenever time and place were fine enough
       for their sport,
And the sun and moon looked upon them with favor.

They threw each other into stinking wells, and fought
       their crazy, giggling way through thorns and mud;
       they rolled around in the yielding sand,
       bruising each other in their unquestioning love.
       Everyone forgave them for everything,
The way you forgive Tuesday for following Monday, the way
You forgive the sun for being just a shade too bright.

When they dyed the governor of Akaba's camel blue and red,
       the whole world seemed suddenly to become
       a mad patchwork of indigo and henna; then,
       for playing a bad joke of me with a snake,
       they fetched water with the women, and almost
Died with shame. I loved them the way I loved fine horses.

Years and years and years ago. And I recall the bullets
Falling in an olive garden where they had played, before
Snake death sucked the nectar from their loins, and
       the whole world turned burnt amber and pale gray.

TOWARDS AKABA

The plan to take her from the north was Auda's;
Her guns faced the sea, anticipating the enemy
        in an element which was not ours. What
        did we have to do with water?
                    Our rivers
Of camels flowed over basalt, over murderous noons
When the violent sun pummelled the world into
        solid light,
           and at night the shivering
        malarial moon considered us with scorn.

On high tides of sand, the nauseous I, a scorpion,
Danced in a slow delirium across the desert
        towards Akaba;
           we drank foul water full of
        dead camels, water with pink blobs on it.
Then, on the sixth of July we splashed into the sea
        at Akaba,
           and for a long time afterwards
I feared to swim, remembering the empty city and
        the naked guns behind us, and the sound
        of waves, delirious against the shore.

NITROGLYCERINE TULIPS

We planted things called tulip bombs to knock out
        Turkish trains, or curl up the tracks;
        the Turks were so stupid, it sometimes
        seemed to me too easy. How could they
        expect a *proper* war
If they gave us no chance to honor them?

I called myself Emir Dynamite, and became quite deft
        at the whole business of organized
        destruction. In the back of one train
        which I derailed, was a carriage full of
        dying men; one whispered *Typhus*,
So I wedged the door closed and left them in.

Another time I straightened out the bodies of dead Turks,
        placing them in rows to look better;
        I was trying, I think, to make it
        a neat war. Once there were three hundred
        of them, with their clothes stripped off,
And I wanted nothing more than to lie down with them,

And die, of course — and think of nothing else but
        raspberries cold with rain, instead of
        sending currents into blasting gelatin
        and watching the sad old trains
        blow sky high
With Turks in little bits flying around everywhere.

SOLAR WIND

It comes upon you unawares—
                            something racing out of the edge
Of your vision, as when you are staring at something
             and not staring — looking through —
A herd of white horses grazing on the periphery
Of your sight, and the afternoon
                        slanting into night—

Comes the wind that is
               the color of the sun, and your eyes
          which are nuggets of gold follow it
          down the barrels of the rifles, through
          the gun-cotton, and over the culverts,
Leaving everything gold, gold in its wake.

The past and the future are burning up; the present
          melts down the middle, a river of wind,
          wind from the sun, gold wind, anything—
And suddenly you know that all mysteries have been solved
          for you, all questions answered.

You must find a god to worship or you will die
In that unholy moment just before darkness and the sound
Of guns.

SOLUTIONS

During one period I judged or cured:
        twelve cases of armed assault
        four camel thefts
        a marriage
        two ordinary thefts
        a divorce
        fourteen feuds
        two cases of Evil Eye
        and one bewitchment.

I cured the bewitchment by casting
        a counter-spell of my own,
The Evil Eyes by staring at their possessors
        with my two horrible blue ones,
And I stopped one feud by executing
        the instigator with my own gun.

The other problems I patched up somehow,
Knowing it was all a pack of lies;
        there were no real
Solutions, anywhere, for anything.

ON THE DAY OF RESURRECTION

On the day of resurrection, all animals
      and inanimate things
      will be given the power of speech.
The sun will rise in the West, and
A monster will arise out of the earth
      in the courtyard of the Kaaba.
It will be twice as tall as Noah's ark,
And will be composed of parts of eleven animals:

      the head of a bull
      the eyes of a hog
      the ears of an elephant
      the horns of a stag
      the neck of a giraffe
      the breast of a lion
      the color of a tiger
      the back of a cat
      the tail of a ram
      the legs of a camel
      the voice of an ass

It will speak Arabic.

MORNING HORSES

The whole war was a play of night and day, of blood
            and light and shadow — night easing in
            on the oiled hooves of the horses,
And day an open wound that stank and oozed.

At midnight the silence, the voluptuous stars, the sweet,
            severe rocks, serene in moonlight. And once
            when the moon was eclipsed (as I alone
            knew it would be)— we took a small village,
Going about our nasty business blindfolded, as it were;
            it was that easy. And another time,
We huddled together around a fire,
            listening to the eloquent speech
            of Allenby's guns in Palestine,
            knowing the war was almost won.

The stories go on and on. Once at dawn when the stars
            were still out, and the ghost-flowers
            of the night were withering, one man came
            to wake me up, saying: *my lord, I am gone blind.*
And then the velvet horses sallied forth to drink again
            the camels' milk, and take us into the noble
            morning.

DERAA

I started to write something like:
The citadels of my integrity were lost, or
   quo vadis from here, Lawrence?
                  How pathetic.
I may as well tell you that as a boy my best castle
   was beseiged and overcome by my brothers.

What happened of course was that I was raped at Deraa,
   beaten and whipped and reduced to shreds
   by Turks with lice in their hair, and VD,
   a gift from their officers, crawling all over
   their bodies.
            I had thought that the Arabs were
Bad enough. Slicing the soles of a prisoner's feet
   so that when they let him return to his men,
   he went very, very slowly;
             but they were merciful.

Imagine, I could never bear to be touched by anybody;
I considered myself a sort of flamboyant monk, awfully
   intact, yet colorful.
           Inviolable is the word.
But everything is shameful, you know; to have a body
   is a cruel joke. It is shameful to be under
   an obligation to anything, even an animal;
   life is shameful; I am shameful. There.

So what part of me lusted after death, as they smashed
       knees into my groin and turned a small knife
       between my ribs? Did I cry out or not when
       they held my legs apart and one of them rode
       upon me, laughing, and splitting open
       a bloody pathway through my soul?
I don't remember.
                   They beat me until something, some
       primal slime spilled out of me, and fire
       shot to my brain.
                   On a razor edge of reality,
I knew I would come out of this, bleeding and broken,
       and singing.

THE REAL ENEMIES

In that land where the soul aged long before the body,
My nameless men, my glamorous bodyguards,
                                        died for me.
My deadly friends with their rouged lips and pretty eyes
            died for me; *my bed of tulips* I called them,
            who wore every color but the white
            that was mine alone to wear.

But they could not guard me against the real enemies —
Omnipotence, and the Infinite—
                            those beasts the soul invents
            and then bows down before.
The real enemies were not the men of Fakhri Pasha, nor
Were they even of this world.
                        One could never conquer them,
Never. Hope was another of them. Hope, most brutal of all.

For those who thought clearly, failure was the only goal.
Only failure could redeem you, there where the soul aged
            long before the body.
You failed at last, you fell into the delicious light
            and were free.

And there was much honor in this;
                            it was a worthy defeat.
Islam is surrender — the passionate surrender of the self,
            the puny self, to God.
We declared a Holy War upon Him and were victors as He won.

THEIR DEATHS

In a horrible winter of snow south of the Dead Sea, we sat,
      white minds around a dying fire,
      and young Daoud died in Akaba
      of whatever evil or fever kills a boy.
The days began and ended when they wanted to, and there
The loud protesting camels proclaimed the end of the world.

The snow was the colour of flesh, of puke, of wisdom,
      of the day after tomorrow;
      that whole winter reeked of death,
      and young Daoud died then in Akaba.
Farraj, in a later time and another place, was shot, and I
Thought of what the Turks would do to his perfect body, so
      I finished off the job with my own gun.

Now they greet me, my little brothers, in a black dream.
      Hello, Daoud; Hello Farraj.
      They lean on the horizon, insolent and wise,
      and my thoughts are tangled in their hair.
Here under sober stars they forgive me everything, and I
Take leave of them politely, turning away to other things,

Remembering how once I was the coolest of men, deserting
A photographer who shot me standing in a group of
      ridiculous cactii, by saying simply:
      I have to go now; they're having a war.

GHAZALA'S FOAL

Ghazala was the second finest camel in all Arabia, and
She did not know it.
She had absolutely no mission in life
and no sense of honor or of shame; she was
almost perfect.
I've seen so many camels die
that it doesn't matter — the females going on
until they foundered and died in their tracks,
the males roaring and flinging themselves down
and dying unnecessarily out of sheer rage, those
we scooped out of the snow at Tafileh — but
Mostly I remember Ghazala's foal, getting up and walking
when it was three hours old, then falling down
again, in a little heap of slippery limbs.

One of the men skinned it, and Ghazala cried and sniffed
the little hide.
Then we marched again, and often
she stopped short, and looked around wildly,
remembering something that was terribly important,
then lapsing into a blank, dazed stare.
Only
when the poor, tiny piece of skin was placed
before her on the ground would she
Murmur something, nudge it, ponder a while, and walk on.

THE DEATH OF DAHOUM

Once I said it was as though you assumed the world
    while you lived, took it upon yourself
    lightly, like a cloak — but now
I think it was the world which borrowed you for a time
And then let go.

No one was there when the world began for you, Dahoum,
    and I was not there when it ended,
    when your lungs filled up with water
    and water filled the dark well of your mouth.
Once I could have drowned in your liquid eyes, forever.

I had this gift for you — the freedom of your race. But
    you come in dreams to tell me
    it was wasted; and in those dreams
    you wear your death well, gracefully.

What would you have said — and in what tongue —
    had you been able, when you died,
    to speak?

TAFAS

We came to the village after the Turks. Everyone was
                                        dead,
Except a little girl who came out from the shadows
                                        with
A fibrous hole gaping where her neck and body joined;
                                                she
Cried *don't hit me, Baba*, then hobbled away and fell

Down in a little heap.
                    And then, I think, she died.

Death's little silver cock was stuck
                        between her mother's legs;
She sat on the tip of a saw
                        bayonet. And a pregnant woman
Was bent over a sheepfold,
                        the hilt of Hell's sword
Sticking up from where
                    the fetus was, into the air.
                                        And others
Were pinned by legs and arms to the ground like
                                        insects
Mounted by an insane collector.
                        We went after the Turks
And killed them all.
                    Then we blew in the heads of the animals.
The sweet salt blood
                of the child ran out and out
                                        and on and on
All the way to Damascus.
                    All this happened as I have said, and
The next day was Friday.

HORSES

Horses. Horses of the dawn,
Shadowy horses, dreaming horses,
Parallel horses, horses at right angles,
Horses of the afternoon and horses of the evening,

Horses who were the custodians of our souls
And kept our mad desires in check—
Bloody horses, stolen horses, gift horses, fallen horses—
I have ridden them all, beasts
                              of the most exalted sun.

Their ghosts are here now; they are
                                      horses of heaven;
They speak to me of midnight and the last dark wadi.

A PHOTOGRAPH FROM CARCEMISH

I gaze at you now, my darling, my brother,
      the pistol asleep in your young groin,
      your lips pulled back in a mighty grin.
My little Hittite, after you there can be no other.

In your dark eyes, my darling, my brother,
The world was created from the waters of Chaos;
      now black waves of tears
      crash upon the beaches of my sleep
      and drown my dreams forever.

Dahoum, Dahoum, Dahoum!

DAMASCUS

The dream was dead in me before we reached Damascus;
        it died with your death, and dead love
Was all I carried around with me in the clumsy luggage
        of the desert. But I remember
Entering the city, and the air silk with locusts;
        there was the smell of eternal cookies baking,
And someone ran up to me with a bunch of yellow grapes.

In the crowds, the Arabs smelled of dried sweat,
        and the English had a hot aura of piss
And naptha. For some reason I noticed a sword
        lying unused in a garden, a still garden
Behind a palm tree. And the worthless Turkish money
        was flying crazily through the air.
Later, in the evening, the satiny white sand cooled
        my feet; nowhere else was there such sand.

That night the Turks and Germans burned what was left
        of their ammunition dumps.
They're burning Damascus, I said. And then I fell asleep.

3
NECESSARY EVILS
Aftermath

THE PEACE CONFERENCE

After prostituting myself in the service of an alien race,
     I was too mangled for politics; the world
     swirled around me and I was its still center.
Old men crawled out from the woodwork and seized upon
     our victory, to re-shape it at their will.
We stammered that we had worked for a new heaven and
     a new earth. They thanked us kindly, and
     made their peace.

France carved up Syria as Feisal questioned their rights
     to do so, inquiring gently which of them
     had won the Crusades;
                    everyone was carving up
     the kingdoms of each other's minds.
I quietly arranged everyone's destiny to my satisfaction,
     without revealing it out loud, as an inner voice
     informed me I had not done well at all —
I had freed the Arabs from everybody but ourselves.

My ideas were simple, always have been; I wanted only:
     an association of free, separate Arab states,
     the beginning of the United States of Arabia,
     the first brown dominion within the Empire,
And no mad talk of Arab unity; no one can unite
     the facets of a jewel.

Everything sickened me; I had been betrayed from the moment
     I was born. I betrayed the Arabs;
     Everything betrays everything.
It was an Arab war, waged and led by Arabs, for an Arab aim
In Arabia, I said, as the bedlam grew louder,
     and France and Britain played chess
     with the world.
                  Feisal caught my eye, saying
Without words: *I've given you my dreams, and now*
     you have to dream them.

TALL TALES

It has been said that I sometimes lie, or bend the truth
          to suit me. Did I make that four hundred mile
          trip alone in Turkish territory or not?
          I wonder if it is anybody's business
          to know. Syria is still there,
          and the long lie that the war was.

Was there a poster of me offering money for my capture,
          and did I stand there staring at myself,
          daring anyone to know me? Consider
          truth and untruth, consider why they call them
          the *theatres* of war. All of us
          played our roles to the hilt.

Poets only play with words, you know; they too
          are masters of the Lie, the Grand Fiction.
          Poets and men like me who fight for something
          contained in words, but not words.

What if the whole show was a lie, and it bloody well was—
          would I still lie to you? Of course I would.

IN THE RANKS

The only things that servicemen see are other servicemen.
   (Trees and starlight and animals. Sometimes.)
Since I am a dangerous man, I hid myself among them,
   so that everything wouldn't kindle around me,
   and the forces I released would stay in check.

In uniform I dreamed of death turned inside out —
   of crustaceans who wear their skeletons
   on the outside. What was beaten out of me
In those absurd drills at dawn, was the insolence
   of simply being. I kept my soul in prison,
For nowhere could it exist in safety, nowhere in the world.

Outside, I was whatever England wanted me to be,
   but in the ranks I was an eager servant
   eating dirt until its taste was normal to me.
In Arabia a slave is more privileged than a servant,
   can spit on his master, and call him by name,
   and eat and sleep with him;
But I wanted no privileges, and subservience was easy.

When I began to enjoy the whippings Bruce bestowed on me,
   I do not know; probably right from the start,
   when I told him I had an uncle who would pay
Him to punish me. He whipped me hard enough that often
   white blood came, my final penitence.
The war was over — (it had been a jolly good war, you know)—
   and now was the time for a raging peace.

THE R.A.F.

Every day the men went up, scaling the heavens
        in a blaze of petrol; there was nothing left
For us but the conquest of the air, and whoever offended
        the men, offended the Air itself.
I rejoiced in building flying boats for air-sea rescues,
        awed by the intricacy of the Machine,
        logical, masculine; there were no women
        in the Machine, in any Machine.

We were civilized and clever; I was sporting one of my
        new names. It seemed that all our efforts
Were devoted to getting mankind, with all its history
        and fragile, terrible dreams,
        off the ground. I suggested that some flier
        Cross the Ruba el Khali, the Empty Quarter in Arabia
        where no man had ever gone,
But someone did it later, overland, without us.

I was happy, and any happiness seemed to be an overdraft
        on life. Does one have a second chance?
Is there a second string to the bow? as Auda would ask.
        No matter. My soul rushed upwards
        if only for a time
        on smoky, blackened wings.

CLOUDS HILL

Over twenty miles of broken heath and a river valley
Full of rhododendrons, the Prince of Mecca comes home.
  At least I think I am at home, but
  even the house is travelling somewhere —
  through time, I think, and beyond.
What is exotic? Home is more exotic than anywhere.
Walking to Clouds Hill, I see the trees get crookeder
  and crookeder; their branches bridge
  the night and morning. Herds of clouds
Erase the sunset; I inhabit the hard core of everywhere.

The wind is easing south; soon, shy stars will come.
Everything has designed itself — the planets know me,
  wind knows me, night knows me;
  Clouds Hill leans against the sky.
I'm awaiting something so important it will never be,
And in dreams I go south and south and south again:
  Damascus, Deraa, Amman, Jerusalem,
  Beersheba, Ma'an, Akaba, Wejh, Um Lej,
  Yenbo, Rabegh, Jidda, Mecca.

Feisal is dead; Bob and Mother are still spreading God,
  and the news from China is nil.
Some of my diaries were written in pencil, upside-down,
  and day after day I decipher them
  on a heavy oak desk.
I live on dark chocolate, and write about the War.

THE VOID

The last truly foolish thing I did was some years ago
When I flew the Hejaz flag from the pinnacle of All Souls;
I knew then that I was becoming an aging schoolboy,
    a master-prig with an ego as big
    as an ostrich egg. A pity,
    for I was still young.

Now I'm gray-haired, half-blind, and shaking at the knees;
There's something almost obscene about the few gold teeth
    I got in nineteen-thirty. What
    have I done, what am I doing, what
    am I going to do?
Days seem to dawn, suns to shine, evenings to follow.
I have burned all my bridges behind me; this is high, dry
    land.

I'm going around shooting the same camel in the head
Over and over; I'm a pilgrim forever circling the Kaaba,
    which has none of its sides or angles equal,
    for whatever that's worth.
Have you ever been a leaf, and fallen from your tree
    in Autumn? It's like that.

Poets put things like shirt-sleeves or oysters
Into their poems, to prevent you from laughing at them
    before they have laughed at themselves.
    I have put an ostrich egg in this one
    to amuse you. I have already laughed.

Where are my noble brothers, my bodyguards, my friends,
Those slender camelmen who rode with me to the ends
    of the desert? When does the great dream end?
    With my right wrist recently broken,
    I write this sad, left-handed poem.

BOANERGES

I call all my grand bikes *sons of thunder*, or
devil-horses, as Auda would have said;
Someone warned me I'd break my neck on my present one.
      I said that's better than dying in bed,
Or walking down some street with its hungry doors
      and falling off the kerb
      into someone else's death.

At the very least I want my death to be my own;
      meanwhile I eat the miles, shape myself
To the flashing contours of the hills, know myself
      to be streets ahead of everyone.
I ride this wild motor-god until my guts explode
      like seeds of dynamite, then
      fizzle out into perfect nothing.

Now every night I pray the lord my soul to keep,
And make sure everything's alive before I go to sleep.

THE DESIRABILITY OF EL AURENS

No matter how much I insist that all through the War
I was Feisal's man — they still want me to be their prince,
      all dressed up in my Sherifian regalia,
      looking like a perfect idiot, posing
      for the cameras, and hating it
      all the way to Damascus.

My past is a tin can tied to the tail of a dog
That rattles whenever he does. A discharged mental patient
      with the face of a wrinkled monkey
      is reported to be impersonating me;
      he's already gone to the zoo, and
      condemned the camels for being mangy.

Many women are in love with someone called El Aurens;
They think they know me, but my name is Legion.
      Two women and four men sent me hideous,
      carnal love letters at Christmas;
      they don't know that one live thing
      can never touch another live thing, and

Intimacy is shameful unless it's perfect. *I* know that.
I also know that el Aurens will never lose his heart—
      that monstrous piece of machinery he abhors.
      Let his several selves enthrall them!
      All the while, he sits in a small cottage
      smiling, and listening to Mozart.

THERE IS NO PLACE TO HIDE

Here is a famous world; I'm standing on a stage
With ten spotlights on me, talking about how I detest
        publicity. I stand there like an ass,
        apologizing for having a past, a soul,
        a name (which one?), and then
        back shyly into the limelight.

No. What I'm really doing is standing in an unlit room
Holding a court martial upon myself. Shaw tells me
        that to live under a cloud
        is to defame God. I can neither reveal myself
        nor hide. No matter what I do, I am naked.
I can clothe myself in silk or chain mail, and I
        am naked; everything shows through
        and yet no one can see me.

Can you imagine that posterity will call me wonderful
        on the basis of a few pencil sketches,
        a revolt in the desert,
        and my irresistably foul soul?
Outside my window, a small tit bird bashes itself
        against the glass. At first I thought
        it was admiring itself in the window.
        Now I know it's mad.

HOT BATHS

All I want now is to boil the Hell out of myself,
       let the elastic water explore me and find
       all my parts guilty of consciousness;
I slide under, wallowing in a world of pure idea
       which both my mind and my body adore.
I feel the heat where one finds poetry — in the hollow
       diaphragm under the cage of ribs.

I whistle. Arabs would say I'm speaking with devils,
       as my various parts burn one by one
       from the elbows to the knees.
I've been burning like this since the day I was born,
       and I'm scalded all over
       and still not clean.
At Mecca, there's a sacred well called the Zem-Zem,
       said to be the direct route to heaven;
       Indian pilgrims, impatient for the journey
       and praying loudly, often jump right in.

NOTES FROM THE DEAD LAND

I have died at last, Feisal. I have been lying
On this hospital bed for five days, and I know
        that I am dead. I was going back home
        on my big bike, and I wasn't doing more
        than sixty when this black van, death camel,
Slid back from the left side of my head, and ahead,
Two boys on little bikes were biking along, and
        something in my head, some brutal music
        played on and on. I was going too fast,
        I was always going too fast for the world,
So I swerved and fell on my stupid head, right
In the middle of the road. I addressed myself
        to the dark hearts of the tall trees
        and nothing answered.

The Arabs say that when you pray, two angels stand
On either side of you, recording good and bad deeds,
        and you should acknowledge them.
        Lying here, I decide that now
        the world can have me any way it pleases.
I will celebrate my perfect death here. *Maktub:*
It is written. I salute both of the angels.

DEPARTURES

Ghostly riders on blonde and dreaming camels
                                         drift
Out of the east side of my sight,
                                harbingers of morning.
I see again the sword in the still
                                garden
Behind the palm tree —
                        Feisal's sword, flashing. The air
Is silk with locusts;
                    then the drawn sword breaks the silk
And the sky heaves
                open.

Night comes and the stars are out. Salaam.